HIDDUIL

HAVE THE BEST DAY OF YOUR LIFE

A 31-DAY DEVOTIONAL

BY

N.J. Matrone

CHOICE PUBLICATIONS

Copyright © 2024 by Nicholas Matrone

All rights reserved.

This book may not be reproduced, in whole or in part, including illustrations, in any form (beyond that copying permitted by Sections 107 and 108 of the U.S. Copyright Law and except by reviewers for the public press), without written permission from the Publisher, Choice Publications LLC

Choicepublications.com

Unless otherwise indicated, all Scripture quotations are from the CSB. Scripture quotations marked CSB have been taken from the Christian Standard Bible®, Copyright © 2017 by Holman Bible Publishers. Used by permission. Christian Standard Bible® and CSB® are federally registered trademarks of Holman Bible Publishers.

HTBDOYL Logo Design by Nick Gaitan

Cover design by N.J. Matrone, Collect & Contrast, and Choice Publications

Interior design by Joseph Lawrence

Set in Georgia font,

ISBN 979-8-9900751-5-3

"Life is like a hot air balloon... You can either ride it or watch it fly away."

In loving memory of Antonio & Theresa Pavone

CONTENTS

INTRODUCTION   **PAGE 11**

DAY 1 THE END	15
DAY 2 THIS IS THE DAY!	19
DAY 3 THE THIRD DAY	21
DAY 4 THE RESURRECTED LIFE	25
DAY 5 NOW IS THE DAY	29
DAY 6 EVEN IF HE DOESN'T	33
DAY 7 WELCOME TO THE JOY MASQUERADE	35
DAY 8 GABRIELLE	39
DAY 9 SELF-LOVE	43
DAY 10 RESIST THE SOUP	45
DAY 11 THE NUMBER ELEVEN	49
DAY 12 HOLY	53
DAY 13 TRUE WORSHIP	57
DAY 14 PEACE BE STILL	59
DAY 15 WITH GREAT POWER	61

DAY 16 THE PURPOSE OF PURPOSE	65
DAY 17 TAKE HEART	69
DAY 18 THE JAILBROKEN WORLD	71
DAY 19 MY ACHY BREAKY HEART	73
DAY 20 HEROES & VILLAINS	75
DAY 21 TAKING UP YOUR MAT	79
DAY 22 SEEK FIRST	83
DAY 23 WONDERLESS	85
DAY 24 MOLDY OR MOLDED?	89
DAY 25 EXITING TEMPTATION STATION	93
DAY 26 SCISSORS TO FEATHERS	97
DAY 27 FIRM FOUNDATION	101
DAY 28 THE GOOD OL DAYS	105
DAY 29 BLESSED	107

DAY 30 MUCH LOVE	109
DAY 31 THE TWO-SIDED COIN	111
THE BEGINNING	113
DAY ZERO	117
ACKNOWLEDGMENTS	119
FROM THE PUBLISHER	123

Howdy!

The fact that you are reading this right now means you have picked up my book – well, that's obvious! Whether you're just reading the introduction to see if this is something you would want to read, or you are sitting down to read it for the first time, I am aware that this could be our only encounter together. So, firstly and most importantly, I just want to tell you this...

Jesus loves you.

This may be something you are being told for the first time, or it could be your gazillionth time being told this good news. Yet, no matter how many times you have been told or haven't been told this... It's a fact that has been true since before your existence and will remain so even after your last breath.

Jesus's love for you isn't based on merit, or what you have done, or didn't do. Jesus's love is simple and true and perfect. But don't take my word for it. Here are His:

For God loved the world in this way: He gave his one and only Son, so that everyone who believes in him will not perish but have eternal life. (John 3:16)

He loves you so much that He gave up His life so that we can truly live ours, with Him, in an everlasting abundance. This is the very purpose of this devotional. No, I don't have every specific answer to every situation, but I know who the answer is. That is my mission in this book: to help point you to the One who has come to give you life and life more abundant.

In Him, have the best day of your life.

P.S. It is so nice meeting you! :)

DAY 1 - THE END

I am the Alpha and the Omega, the first and the last, the beginning and the end. (Revelation 22:13)

Yes! You read the title right! This is the end. The book is over, and you can put it down already and move on.

Just kidding! Please stay...

To have the best day of your life every day, you must simply know that the one who made it is already at the end of it. God is the beginning and the end. This one, simple truth has brought me everlasting peace, even when the worst circumstances of life come my way. Challenging circumstances come up in life all the time.

If we're not careful, we can allow them to steal the joy that a new day always brings. It's not difficult to think about the problems a new day can bring: It may be a financial problem; a marital problem; maybe your child draws on your brand new beautiful

THE END

white painted wall with a permanent marker. Have you ever thought about all the gifts that come with a brand-new day? Whatever the circumstances of your morning may be, don't let them steal the thunder of this beautiful new day that our Heavenly Father has made for us. He made it for us to draw nearer to Him.

In order to see each day as the present from God that it is, we must have a simple yet fundamental change in our perspective.

All the problems that come up on a daily basis, that often takes us by surprise, does not surprise God. He is the Alpha and the Omega. He knew the end before there was even a beginning. His ways are not our ways. So what feels like a storm to us is really a lesson to Him, that is teaching us to feel His peace like we have never felt before. Going through the fire means being refined and coming out a new creation.

What the enemy means for evil, God turns to good. The victory is already won. So, all you have to do today – and every day – is to remind yourself to take a deep breath, slow

THE END

down, be still and know that He is God. You can try that with me right now.

Simply breath in as deep as you can through your nose and say, "Thank you God for this day that you have made."

Would you try that with me? Would you make the whole purpose of this day to draw nearer to Him and give Him all of the Glory?

Lastly, take the time to say this simple prayer for your Day 1:

"Lord, this day is a gift from you. I am thankful that you are God, and I am not. You are bigger than the biggest mountain and know all my days before they happen. No circumstance will steal my praise from you. No situation will steal the joy that you have wrapped this present day in! I love you and am so thankful for the opportunity to draw nearer to you, the God of it all!

Amen!"

DAY 2 - THIS IS THE DAY!

This is the day that the Lord has made; we will rejoice & be glad in it. (Psalm 118:24)

Are you having the best day of your life?

This was my "slogan", my mantra, that I lived by and told everyone at my college campus. Why was I doing this? Well, I was just bored with that usual...

"Hey, how are you?"

"Good, how are you?"

"Good, have a great day!"

...That we hear every day. Instead, when someone would ask me how I was doing I would say:

"I'm having the best day of my life!"

That simple switch up in conversation has led to so many opportunities to know people & minister into their lives. It also has, on the other hand, made people annoyed... That's okay – in each case, it was memorable!

THIS IS THE DAY!

Let me ask you a question about this question... When I ask you, what is the best day of your life, what do you imagine? Maybe you think of your wedding day, or the day you start your dream job, or it's the day that you finally make it. We as humans have the tendency to measure a day by its circumstances. For example, a good day is when good things happen to me. A bad day is when bad things happen.

That is not what the psalmist does. Instead, the psalmist reminds us that this day, no matter the circumstances it may hold, is a gift from God. I want to challenge you today to not allow the circumstances of today dictate whether the day is good or bad. Today is the best day ever because God created it, and it's the only day we get to live in presently. Every day is another day to love God and to be loved by Him. What could be better than that?

Prayer:

God, thank you for this day that you have created. It is the best day of my life because you, the one who created it, are with me through every moment and circumstance. Have your way today in your day!

DAY 3 - THE THIRD DAY

For I delivered to you as of first importance what I also received: that Christ died for our sins in accordance with the Scriptures, that he was buried, that he was raised on the third day in accordance with the Scriptures, and that he appeared to Cephas, then to the twelve. (1 Corinthians 15:3-5)

Let's spend the third day of our devotional talking about what happened on the third day after Jesus was crucified on the cross. You may be thinking, what does this have to do with me having the best day of my life?

Everything!

Let me explain... bear with me for a little while today. When Jesus died on the cross, it wasn't because He had done something wrong. No, He was in fact totally innocent. Why then did He have to die in such a way?

THE THIRD DAY

The answer is found in a book of the Old Testament called Isaiah. Isaiah was a prophet who foresaw the sufferings of Jesus. Isaiah 53: 4-5 says:

Surely he took up our pain and bore our suffering, yet we considered him punished by God, stricken by him, and afflicted. But he was pierced for our transgressions, he was crushed for our iniquities; the punishment that brought us peace was on him, and by his wounds we are healed. We all, like sheep, have gone astray, each of us has turned to our own way; and the LORD has laid on him the iniquity of us all.

That sounds very sad! How could we have the best day ever when someone is suffering so terribly for our sakes? It's because Jesus took our place. He took the wrath we deserved. He was broken so that through His death and Resurrection we would be made whole.

THE THIRD DAY

Jesus was raised from the dead. The disappointment of Friday became the celebration of Sunday. What a difference a day can make! The good news is, when Jesus rose from the grave, so did we!

Prayer:

Thank you, Lord, for sending your son to throw my sins in the sea of forgetfulness so that I can live a resurrected life in you. You have made me new, help me to live today like I am brand new. Amen.

DAY 4 - THE RESURRECTED LIFE

First, please take a moment to ponder these two passages of scripture:

My goal is to know him and the power of his resurrection and the fellowship of his sufferings, being conformed to his death, assuming that I will somehow reach the resurrection from among the dead. Not that I have already reached the goal or am already perfect, but I make every effort to take hold of it because I also have been taken hold of by Christ Jesus. Brothers and sisters, I do not consider myself to have taken hold of it. But one thing I do: Forgetting what is behind and reaching forward to what is ahead, I pursue as my goal the prize promised by God's heavenly call in Christ Jesus. Therefore, let all of us who are mature think this way. And if you think differently about anything, God will reveal this also to you. In any case, we should live up to whatever truth we have attained. Join in imitating me, brothers and sisters, and pay careful attention to those who live according to the example you have in us. For I have often told you, and now say again with tears, that many live as enemies of the cross of Christ. Their end is destruction; their god is their stomach; their glory is in their shame; and they are focused on earthly things. Our citizenship is in heaven, and we eagerly wait for a Savior from there, the Lord Jesus Christ. He will transform the body of our humble condition into the likeness of his glorious body, by the power that enables him to subject everything to himself. (Philippians 3:10-21)

Calling the crowd along with his disciples, he said to them, "If anyone wants to follow after me, let him deny himself, take up his cross, and follow me. For whoever wants to save his life will lose it, but whoever loses his life because of me and the gospel will save it. For what does it benefit someone to gain the whole world and yet lose his life? What can anyone give in exchange for his life? For whoever is ashamed of me and my words in this adulterous and sinful generation, the Son of Man will also be ashamed of him when he comes in the glory of his Father with the holy angels." (Mark 8:34-38)

To me, these two passages exemplify what it means to live the resurrected life. They tell me what a life in Christ means better than my own words could ever say. They tell me that Jesus is the way, the truth, and the life. These words, the Word, tells me that Jesus is life and life more abundant, and through Him, we are raised to life anew.

What does this life anew look like?

I want to answer that question with a quote. I don't know who originally wrote this, but it has stuck with me ever since I first read it.

The saying goes, "Know Jesus, know peace.

No Jesus, no peace."

A life anew in Jesus is a life of peace.

#Facts.

Prayer: *Lord, I have read these scriptures today and ask that you will make your resurrection life real to me. Here I am, take these broken pieces and make me new. I want to live this resurrection life in you. I receive it now in Jesus' name. Let my life be proof of your resurrection power & unconditional love.*

Amen.

DAY 5 - NOW IS THE DAY

For He says: "In an acceptable time I have heard you, And in the day of salvation I have helped you." Behold, now is the accepted time; behold, now is the day of salvation. (2 Corinthians 6:2)

Consider again that one phrase:

"I have heard you."

I know deep down in my Spirit that these words are meant for you. He has seen and kept every one of your tears... He was there on your darkest day, just as He was there on your brightest. He has never left you & will never leave you nor forsake you.

As we have discussed before, Jesus not only died and rose again for the forgiveness of our sins. Did you know that He also died so that His Holy Spirit could be poured out to restore the right relationship between God and man?

God has given us Power over death, hell, and the grave, through the precious blood of Jesus, the same blood that has declared us heirs of the living & reigning almighty God. As good as this good news is, it does not mean we will not suffer. In fact, we are called to suffer with Christ. Remember yesterday how we read that Christ calls us to take up our own cross and follow Him?

There is still pain. There is still a lurking, very cunning devil who seeks to steal, kill and destroy us. Still, Jesus encourages us and commands us to, *"Take heart; for I have overcome the world."* (John 16:33) There is no sin too great nor no mountain of sorrows too big to separate you from the love of God. Our biggest hurdle is ourselves.

It's our choice. Either we can pick up our cross and die to ourselves (our sinful nature), or choose to gain the world but lose our soul (our inner spirit). Friend, if I don't give you this opportunity to make that choice now, the rest of this devotional is for nothing. Jesus says:

"I have come to give you life and life more abundant." (John 10:10)

Having the best day of your life is living the more abundant life in Christ Jesus. Life with Him is real life, real joy. There are no tricks or games, just real love.

Friend, I want to pray with you, because now is the day of your salvation. As we pray together, know that these words are not some magic spell that makes life easy and stress free. Rather, as 1 John 1:9 the scripture says; *"If we confess our sins, he is faithful and just and will forgive us our sins and purify us from all unrighteousness."*

That's it, that's all it takes. We must simply make our confession before our savior that we need Him. We then invite Him to have His way in our heart, minds, souls, and lives. Please pray with me:

"God, Here I am with all that I am. With every sin and regret, as well as with every great accomplishment and talent that I have; I lay it all at your feet. Thank you for forgiving me of my sins and I receive that today… I am… a new creation at the hand of the great I AM. My life is yours, let your will be done. In Jesus name. Amen."

Now that we've prayed together, continue to seek Him in prayer and in His word. This devotional can help you do that. I pray that at the end of this devotional you would have developed a pattern in studying God's word.

NOW IS THE DAY

This devotional is 31 days and not 365 days. That's because this devotional is meant as a resource to create a monthly habit of reading the Word and pursuing God. This devotional is meant to point those who read it to the real and Holy word of God, the Bible.

Jesus is our best day ever, and He is the one that is eternal.

DAY 6 – EVEN IF HE DOESN'T

Shadrach, Meshach and Abednego replied to him, "King Nebuchadnezzar, we do not need to defend ourselves before you in this matter. If we are thrown into the blazing furnace, the God we serve is able to deliver us from it, and he will deliver us from Your Majesty's hand. But even if he does not, we want you to know, Your Majesty, that we will not serve your gods or worship the image of gold you have set up." (Daniel 3:16-18)

Look at the beginning of verse 18 again: *"Even if he does not…"*

This bold statement says it all.

So often, as Christians, we can have the false view that God is some kind of genie that grants our every wish. He's not. He's a King. The King.

We must worship Him every day, not because of what He has, can, or might do for us, but because He's God and He alone is worthy of all our praise. What makes this day so good is that He made it. God is our waymaker and miracle worker. Whatever you are believing for today, He is able and all powerful. He can do all things, but even if He does not do all things as you expect them to be done.... Even if that miracle you are praying for doesn't come....

...Will you still praise Him and not bow down to the idols of this world?

Prayer:

God, you alone are worthy of my praise! I thank you for all that you have blessed me with. I believe that you are able to provide for all that I'm believing for, but even if you don't... my life is yours. You are my sovereign King, have your way and let your will be done on Earth as it is in heaven.

DAY 7 - WELCOME TO THE JOY MASQUERADE

"For everything there is a season, and a time for every matter under heaven: a time to be born, and a time to die; a time to plant, and a time to pluck up what is planted; a time to kill, and a time to heal; a time to break down, and a time to build up; a time to weep, and a time to laugh; a time to mourn, and a time to dance; a time to throw away stones, and a time to gather stones together; a time to embrace, and a time to refrain from embracing; a time to seek, and a time to lose; a time to keep, and a time to throw away; a time to tear, and a time to sew; a time to keep silence, and a time to speak; a time to love, and a time to hate; a time for war, and a time for peace"

(Ecclesiastes 3:1-8)

One common misconception that can be formed from receiving this free gift of salvation and living the Resurrected life is that once we know Jesus, there will be no more pain. Once a storm comes, some are completely appalled and may even think the salvation they have received is a fallacy. There can also be this false sense that everything has to be happy, bright, and perfect. Then, once there is a hint of darkness, despair, pain, rejection, and a rain cloud in sight... There comes the complaint, "This isn't what I signed up for."

In spite of imperfection, some pick up the mask of joy to hide any ounce of noticeable pain to look the part for the Church and other Christians. I've been there.

Later, I was encouraged so by the word above, that there is a time for mourning. It's okay to mourn. The idea of having the best day of your life isn't always living on a field with sunflowers and dandelions.

"I don't say this out of need, for I have learned to be content in whatever circumstances I find myself. I know how to make do with little, and I know how to make do with a lot. In any and all circumstances I have learned the secret of being content— whether well fed or hungry, whether in abundance or in need. I am able to do all things through him who strengthens me. Still, you did well by partnering with me in my hardship." (Philippians 4:11-14)

In this letter to the Church at Philippi, Paul was vulnerable. He recognized his moments of hunger, his moments of little, and the circumstances he faced weren't something to hide from; rather he boasted that he can do all things through Him. Although the joy of the Lord is our strength; It's coming to an understanding that there is darkness in the world, but the light of Jesus shines through it all. Yes, there is a time for mourning, but with that comes the time of Joy. The Resurrection life recognizes that there is a physical death, but it also rejoices in the truth that death is defeated and that there is victory over the grave through the death & resurrection of our Lord & Savior Jesus Christ. He has prepared a place for His children in eternity with Him.

Let's all donate any mask hidden in the wardrobe of our souls to the spiritual thrift store and become the new creation that God has called us to be. We are called to be Christ-like, not participators in the joy masquerade.

Prayer:

Lord, If there has been any mask that I've been wearing, I lay it down. You have given me an identity in you. You said we will have challenges in this world through your word, but you also said to take heart. Today, help me to truly walk in Resurrection power, but to not live under a fake facade of perfection. Teach me to live like you and to be honest with myself with things that I must change and wounds that I need to come to you with for healing.

Here I am, maskless and pride abandoned so that you may have your way with me.

Amen.

DAY 8 - GABRIELLE

I will praise thee; for I am fearfully and wonderfully made: marvelous are thy works; and that my soul knoweth right well. (Psalms 139:14)

I am dedicating this day of our devotional to my sister, for reasons that she knows. This devotional may have never been finished if it wasn't for her and many others' encouragement and belief in what God is going to do through it.

The verse we are reading today is a verse that she has tattooed on herself. Today's verse is deeply meaningful to both my sister and I. It has changed both of our lives. This verse speaks to one battle of the soul that I believe we all commonly face. This battle can be encapsulated in one question we often ask ourselves:

Are we worth it?

Our American culture, in the era we are living in, can be so biased towards outward appearances. Our culture calls us to covet our money, dress for success, and obsess over

GABRIELLE

what we look like. No wonder we have grown up caring so much about our looks.

I would often look in the mirror and be disgusted at who was staring back at me. No matter what clothes or hairstyle I had, I always felt reflected by a feeling of emptiness. "Isn't it good looks that win the hearts of women?", I would ask myself. I would also tell myself, "If I don't have that, then I'm not enough."

I know now that I'm not the only one who has wrestled with these thoughts and self perceptions. Let me tell you a story:

Once, I was watching the lion king again because it was my favorite Disney movie growing up. In that beautifully crafted movie, a deep revelation hit me right in my soul. There is a scene in which Simba ran into Rafiki the baboon. Rafiki tells Simba that his father is alive. Although Simba was in disbelief, he still didn't reject the chance to hope, trusting even in the ounce of possibility of seeing his father again. Rafiki ran into the forest, and Simba followed. Beyond the forest was a lake. Rafiki pointed to the body of water and told him to look, that's where Simba's father was. Simba, still in disbelief, looked and was disappointed.

He only saw his own reflection. Rafiki then said, look closer. Simba looked again and, as the ripples cleared, began to see the reflection of his father.

This scene wrecked me. I ran into the bathroom right after to look in the mirror again, but this time to look closer. What did I see?

My friend, you are made in the image of the one true King. You are wonderful and fearfully made by the hands of the creator of the here, now, and beyond. Next time you look in the mirror and don't like what you see... Look closer.

Prayer:

God, what an honor it is to be made in your image and likeness. Today, I choose to see myself and everyone I meet with your eyes. You see so much more than what our eyes see. Forgive me for the words and thoughts I have used to discredit your creation and help me in the future to recognize any attack of insecurity used by the enemy to take my eyes off you. I will praise you; for I am fearfully and wonderfully made: marvelous are your works; and that my soul knows it well.

Amen.

DAY 9 - SELF LOVE

We love because he first loved us.
(1 John 4:19)

Our American culture today puts us at center stage. Self-love. That's the buzzword. The idea seems practical, and in no way or form am I saying loving yourself is bad. Just look at the previous day. I am asking, though, how can we love ourselves if we don't first know what love is?

What is true love?

We often get glimpses of love through Disney movies, tv shows, and the seemingly endless love stories that are unraveled around us. Even with all this love in the air, divorces still exist. We all have had our unfair share of heartbreak in a relationship of some kind, whether romantically, or in family, or between friendships. Unfortunately, hurt people hurt people. The cycle continues. How then can we love if we don't even know what true love is for ourselves?

You might be saying, great! Now you got me even more confused on what love is.

SELF LOVE

Does love even exist?

No need to fear, friend. Perfect love is here, and it casts out all fear. The apostle Paul tells us what true love is:

Love is patient, love is kind. Love does not envy, is not boastful, is not arrogant, is not rude, is not self-seeking, is not irritable, and does not keep a record of wrongs. Love finds no joy in unrighteousness but rejoices in the truth. It bears all things, believes all things, hopes all things, endures all things. (1 Corinthians 13:4-7)

God is Love. God loves you. Put that together and... Love loves you. In accepting His love and being transformed by it, we learn how to truly love ourselves and others. Here is your prayer for today:

God, thank you for being perfect love in a world that tries to love without you and so only creates a counterfeit. You're my real thing in this world full of fakes and lies. I surrender my heart, and in this moment, please allow the truth of your love to wash and cleanse me. I want to experience true love today, right now, in your perfect presence.

Amen.

DAY 10 - RESIST THE SOUP

They exchanged the truth about God for a lie and worshiped and served created things rather than the Creator—who is forever praised. Amen. (Romans 1:25-26)

Hunger can make people do desperate things!

The term "hangry" exists for a reason. Just like the Hulk said, (*Insert Intimidating Hulk voice here.) "You won't like me when I'm hangry"

Hunger affects the way we think and act. Have you ever seen the Snickers commercial of the person acting like they are in a drama, very dramatically, and then the very kind friend gives them a snicker bar, reciting the famous line, "Dude, You're not you when you're hungry."?

Although it is hilarious, it is also so true. Hunger really puts us in a daze that makes us forget who and whose we are. We see this clearly in the story of Esau and Jacob. This story is found in Genesis 25:19-34. These two brothers were rivals since their shared birth.

RESIST THE SOUP

Jacob was always looking for ways to usurp the "birthright" from his 5-second older brother. One day, Esau had gone out hunting in the woods. When Esau returned, he was hungry... I mean really really hungry! Esau was hangry beyond belief, and Jacob knew that and was waiting for him with his 5-star chef soup of the day. Esau wanted to devour that soup so bad that he was willing to do anything for it. Anything!

"AnyyyyyThinnnnggggg?", Jacob sneered. (That's what Jacob must of said right?)

Then Jacob made his intentions clear. What did he really want in exchange for the soup?

Esau's Birthright.

What does that mean? Well, being the firstborn back then was a big deal. Esau stood to inherit the entirety of his father Isaac's wealth. Jacob, being the second born, was at a huge disadvantage, but he used what he had to come on top. From Jacob's hand, Esau took the soup.

He decided to prioritize his hunger over protecting his birthright. Hunger goes beyond just food. Hunger can be for lust of the flesh, hunger for money and fame. If we're not careful, we too can take the soup.

RESIST THE SOUP

However, when we are born again, allowing God to make us a new creation, we are given a birthright, one that the enemy is jealous of, and his goal as the thief is to rob you of the life more-abundant God has planned for you. My call to action to you today is this:

Resist The Soup!

It may look appetizing, and it may satisfy your hungry urge for a moment, but it won't last forever, and it's not worth giving up your birthright for. Instead, eat the bread of life that satisfies every longing of the soul. Living the best day ever is living every day free from bondage, guilt, and shame. Live today like you are a King's Kid who knows his birthright in God. That's worth more than any flavor of Campbell's soup! Don't exchange the Truth for a lie.

Prayer:

God, today I choose to resist the soup. I choose you alone. You satisfy every longing of my heart. Renew my mind and give me the strength, through your Holy Spirit, to resist any temptation from the enemy. I will not be blinded by the flesh; I am free, in you, from any form of bondage. Today I choose to live life, and life more abundant.

DAY 11 - THE NUMBER ELEVEN

Therefore, a man shall leave his father and his mother and hold fast to his wife, and they shall become one flesh. That is why a man leaves his father and mother and is united to his wife, and they become one flesh. (Genesis 2:24)

On this day, I want to talk about relationships.

You may be wondering, what do relationships have to do with having the best day of your life?

I have asked myself the same question. I have come to find, in my own experiences being a hopeless romantic, that the idea of finding love and my soulmate has consumed the majority of my attention. My longing for a partner became so strong that at the age of 24, I thought my life would never start. Then, suddenly, I was blessed with being in a two-year relationship that unfortunately ended in a failed engagement.

I say I was "blessed" because I grew and learned so much from that experience. The

THE NUMBER ELEVEN

most important thing I took away from that relationship is this: the number eleven.

What does that mean?

Before explaining, let's take another look at today's verse.

God created one whole man and one whole woman. Very easy math there. The hard to grasp concept is how He took two whole beings and made them themselves to be one. The reason I say it's hard to grasp is because, growing up, I had this idea that I would be complete when I find my "other half", and if I never found my other half, I would be incomplete and meaningless. Wasn't I made to be a husband and a father? If I don't become either of those, is my life worth anything?

I know that I'm not the only one who has asked themselves that or something similar.

So, what does the number 11 mean today? The beauty of the number 11 is that it is two complete 1's that have come together to equal a higher value than they could ever achieve on their own. Like this, it is God who makes us whole.

Jesus died for our sins and rose from the grave so that He could have a relationship with us! He does this through His Holy Spirit (see the book of Acts, chapter 2). Therefore, we are never alone, and in Him we lack nothing. A spouse doesn't complete us, but rather, a spouse helps us accomplish God's plans through our lives.

I wasted so much time in my life crying over my singleness when I could have been using it for God's purposes. If that has been you too, rest in the truth that you are complete in the One who has formed you. He knows the plans He has for you. Use this time of singleness, or even if you're on the opposite side of this spectrum, use your relationship in the same way to glorify God and to serve His Kingdom.

Prayer:

God, I want to thank you for being my one and first love. In you I have the longings of my soul. My life is in your hands and that includes "my love life". Today, I surrender that specific desire of my heart because all I want is for your will to be done through my life, howsoever that looks like.

Amen.

DAY 12 - HOLY

Therefore, with your minds ready for action, be sober-minded and set your hope completely on the grace to be brought to you at the revelation of Jesus Christ. As obedient children, do not be conformed to the desires of your former ignorance. But as the one who called you is holy, you also are to be holy in all your conduct; for it is written, Be holy, because I am holy. If you appeal to the Father who judges impartially according to each one's work, you are to conduct yourselves in reverence during your time living as strangers. For you know that you were redeemed from your empty way of life inherited from your ancestors, not with perishable things like silver or gold, but with the precious blood of Christ, like that of an unblemished and spotless lamb. He was foreknown before the foundation of the world but was revealed in these last times for you. Through him you believe in God, who raised him from the dead and gave him glory, so that your faith and hope are in God. (1 Peter 1:13-21)

HOLY

I would be doing a disservice to you, the reader, if I wrote a book about having the best day ever if I didn't talk about Holiness, and how detrimental it can be to pursue perfect, right living. John 10:10 says, *A thief comes only to steal and kill and destroy. I have come so that they may have life and have it in abundance.*

Oftentimes, Christianity is seen as a mere religion stuffed with rules that limits one's freedom or fun. Christianity calls us to be Holy as God is Holy.

But isn't that impossible?

Holiness is more than just an unattainable expectation of perfection. It is really an invitation to being who God has truly designed you to be. God formed and created you. He knows everything about you, even to the place of calling your hair by number.

He even knows our weaknesses too.

There's a reason why we struggle with a lot of the same things people struggled with thousands of years ago in the times of the Bible. That is why God has given us commandments, not to limit our freedom and fun, but so that we can truly live life in abundance, in true freedom and great joy.

Living Holy is living for God and allowing Him to mold you every single day that you are gifted with.

Prayer:

God, I thank you for your call to us to be Holy as you are. You know me better than myself and you know my weakness. Today, make me more like you. Wash me and cleanse me because all I want to do with this day and my life is to please & glorify you. Amen.

DAY 13 - TRUE WORSHIP

Therefore, brothers and sisters, in view of the mercies of God, I urge you to present your bodies as a living sacrifice, holy and pleasing to God; this is your true worship. (Romans 12:1-2)

"This is your true worship," ... That verse hit me hard. I used to see true worship as how passionate and consistently I could sing and dance for God. I saw it even as how much worship music I played in my free time. I had worship music on, so I must be worshiping God right? I was singing at the parts I know, so I must be a worshiper of God – right?

Right?! Wrong...

Instead, Romans 12 shows us that a true and genuine worship to God is simply the way we live our life. When we love Him so much that we want to turn our backs on anything and everything that displeases Him, that's true worship. That is to live Holy and upright for God. That includes singing worship music! Singing is a form of worship that musters all our affection and

TRUE WORSHIP

attention and puts it on the King of Kings and Lord of Lords.

Our worship flows from our heart. In Jeremiah 17:9-10, it tells us the heart is deceitful above all things. We can worship God with all of heart through singing and praise, but if our life preaches another message, it's just songs. Worship is our actions. Faith without works is dead (James 2:6). Therefore, let our song flow from how we live our lives for God, to worship Him in Spirit & in truth.

Prayer:

God,

Thank you for everything you have done for me. I want the way I live the present to be a present unto you. Teach me, Holy Spirit, what it truly means to worship you in Spirit and in Truth. Take my deceitful heart and form it to be more like you, Holy as you are Holy.

Amen.

DAY 14 - PEACE BE STILL

He said to them, "Why are you afraid, you of little faith?" Then he got up and rebuked the winds and the sea, and there was a great calm. (Matthew 8:26)

Have you ever had a day where everything and everyone in your life is against you? A moment where you had no idea how you were going to see another day?

Jesus' disciples once found themselves in a moment just like that. They were on a boat on the sea of Galilee when out of nowhere they were caught in a massive storm. Waves crashed in on their little fisher's boat from all sides. Lightning struck in the sky. Thunder roared. Sharks – oh my! Okay, maybe not sharks, but you know what I mean: it was very scary. They were in a bad spot.

They were afraid. What did they do in the midst of that storm, that fear?

They went to the best possible place, the place where Jesus was. They woke Him up, sharing, more so freaking out, about their situation and the circumstances surrounding them. It wasn't that Jesus didn't know about the storm. It was just that He knew that He is bigger than any storm. He rebuked the disciples, addressing them as, "you of little faith". He then spoke to the waves and the storm, "Peace be still.", instantly, the storm ceased.

Do you know that when you invite the Holy Spirit into your life, the same power that lives in Him, lives in you?

It is so easy to be wavered by the waves around us, pulled by the tides of stress and fear. As a believer, we must come to the revelation of not only who we are, but who lives in us. We aren't slaves to the waves, but the waves are at the mercy of the One who parted the red sea. Use your staff, friend. Like Moses. Pick it up and slam it down in authority over the battlefield of the enemy in your life. Speak to it, say, "Peace be still."

Prayer:

Whatever the waves are in my life, I speak to it right now, peace be still! Thank you, Jesus, for being the one who is bigger than any storm that could ever form! You're bigger. It's you who I trust. It is you who is the King of Peace.

DAY 15 - WITH GREAT POWER...

He also who had received the one talent came forward, saying, 'Master, I knew you to be a hard man, reaping where you did not sow, and gathering where you scattered no seed, so I was afraid, and I went and hid your talent in the ground. Here, you have what is yours.' But his master answered him, 'You wicked and slothful servant! You knew that I reap where I have not sown and gather where I scattered no seed? Then you ought to have invested my money with the bankers, and at my coming I should have received what was my own with interest. So take the talent from him and give it to him who has the ten talents. For to everyone who has will more be given, and he will have an abundance. But from the one who has not, even what he has will be taken away. And cast the worthless servant into the outer darkness. In that place there will be weeping and gnashing of teeth.'

(Matthew 25:24-30)

In this passage, Jesus is sharing a parable that inspires us to take what He has given us

WITH GREAT POWER

and use it. This is a foreshadow of what happens in Matthew 28, when Jesus gives us the great commission, sending His disciples out to make believers of all nations. God gave us the greatest gift of all time, the sacrificial lamb, His son, who died and rose again so that God can pour His Spirit out on us, bringing us to a place of constant communion with our Creator. Now that we have the gift of living with God, what are we doing with it?

There is a quote from a hardly known Marvel story that goes a little like this...

> "With great power comes great responsibility." - Stan Lee

(I hope you can decipher my sarcasm.)

God has given us great power over death, hell, and the grave. Power to see blind eyes open & deaf ears hear. Power to see the lost find new life in God. We are responsible for that power, for the blessings and gifts that God has given us. I challenge you today to ask yourself this...

Am I using the power of my salvation to help save lives by pointing people to the One in whom our salvation is found?

Prayer:

Thank you, God, for the gift of Salvation and the price you paid for me to have it. Lord, I long to do your will, help me to realize even more and grow in the power that you have given me through your Spirit. Fill me today and use me for your glory.

Amen.

DAY 16 - THE PURPOSE OF PURPOSE

"Meaningless! Meaningless!"
  says the Teacher.
"Utterly meaningless!
  Everything is meaningless."
(Ecclesiastes 1:1)

Meaningless...

In the process of writing this devotional, that's how I've been feeling. Meaningless. At 28 years old, I have been heartbroken, am currently jobless, and moved back home with my parents in hopes of a fresh start.

Two weeks after the move, I thought I would feel differently. I thought I would recover, but there was still an overwhelming sensation of feeling... Stuck. As I looked through possible job opportunities and career paths, I was left with the same heart-rending cry as the author of Ecclesiastes...

Meaningless! Everything is meaningless.

If we're not careful, purpose can be used as a weapon against us.

THE PURPOSE OF PURPOSE

What do I mean?

Well, the enemy (Satan) is here to steal, kill, and destroy. If someone does not see the point of living, they are missing their purpose. Have you ever felt that way? Have you ever felt a feeling like your whole life was trapped in a deep pit? This is an existential crisis that is exactly where the enemy of God wants you to be. But that is not where God wants you to be. This is who God says you are.

You are His creation, the masterpiece of the most High King. He has sent you His son, and His son has come to give you life and life more abundant. What does that life more abundant look like?

Life more abundant is more than just pursuing your many purposes, the myriad of meanings we make for ourselves, whatever it is: having a family, working until retirement, or making a ton of money to live a comfortable life. Life more abundant is more meaningful than these temporary things. Life abundant is about the One who defines true purpose, Jesus.

If you ever feel that your life is meaningless, then do what I once did.

Listen to the voice of meaning Himself saying, *"Come to me all who are weary and heavy laden, and I will give you rest."* (Matthew 11:28)

I conclude by urging you the reader (and myself the writer) that instead of chasing purposes, sit at His feet and rest. Pour out your heart and lay all the heavy stuff at His feet.

Prayer:

Lord, here I am with my broken pieces. I give them to you in exchange for your Purpose. You are my purpose. You are bringing meaning into the meaningless. The rest of my days are yours. Have your way. I love you, and I pray the rest of my days show you just that.

Amen.

DAY 17 - TAKE HEART

"I have told you these things, so that in me you may have peace. In this world you will have trouble. But take heart! I have overcome the world." (John 16:33)

After reading this verse you may be thinking, "Great! I read this book to start living the best days of my life, and now you're saying that I will have trouble!"

Well, before anyone asks for a refund... Know this: This verse holds two tremendous keys to your life.

The first key is *acceptance*.

What do we need acceptance of?

That life is life. We live in a fallen world that was poisoned by sin. Although it's been tainted and polluted at the hand of sin... God's thumbprint is undeniable and irrevocable.

The second key is *knowledge of the promise*.

Let Jesus' words, "Take Heart", become tied upon your heart. Rest in His promise that

TAKE HEART

through His death and resurrection, Jesus has overcome the world.

He is the answer for anxiety.

He is the answer for heartbreak

He is the answer for depression.

He is the answer.

Prayer:

God, you know every problem and situation that I'm going through. Today, I am making the decision to take heart and rest on your promise that you have overcome the world and every problem that I'm faced with. My trust is yours.

DAY 18 - THE JAILBROKEN WORLD

They exchanged the truth about God for a lie and worshiped and served created things rather than the Creator—who is forever praised. Amen. (Romans 1:25)

For today's devotional, I want to go more in depth to what was discussed yesterday, on our acceptance that we live in a fallen world.

We live in the jailbroken world.

I find this topic extremely important, because the fact we live in an imperfect world, created by a perfect creator, may raise some questions as to why is our world the way that it is? How is such a bad world possible if God is such a good God?

To answer this question the best that I can, I am going to use a simple example. The example of an iPhone. The most popular cell phone ever created is the iPhone by Apple, which was founded by Steve Jobs.

It was created with its own intended purpose and wrapped in the identity of Apple. When the phone was released, its limitations were

THE JAILBROKEN WORLD

recognized. A reach beyond its limitations was desired. One day, the ability to "Jailbreak" that iPhone became possible. What jailbreaking your iPhone would grant the user was the freedom to download whatever that user wanted…. Against the will of its creator.

That's like the world we live in today. Our world is one that has been jailbroken, one where we as a people have denied the will of our Creator to pursue our own desires, and the outcome of that is what we live in today. The "rules" God has laid before us in the Bible isn't to withhold our freedom, but to protect us from the taint of sin.

My challenge to you today is to simply reflect on this question, "Have you exchanged the truth for a lie?"

Prayer:

God, reveal anything in me that displeases you and wash me from any taint of the world. You have placed me here for a period of time, but my home is with you for eternity. I lay this day at your feet and will live today delighting in your truth. Amen.

DAY 19 - MY ACHY BREAKY HEART

"The heart is deceitful above all things, And desperately wicked; Who can know it? I, the LORD, search the heart, test the mind, Even to give every man according to his ways, According to the fruit of his doings." (Jeremiah 17:9-10)

Have you ever heard the phrase, "Trust your heart"?

You may have even said this phrase at some point in your life, perhaps screaming it from the mountaintops whilst blaring cinematic music, "I choose to follow my heart!"

No, you've never done that?

Well, regardless I think we all have or will come to that place where our heart's burn with passion and we follow its direction, whether that's to a dream job, dream spouse, or even dream car. As friends, we can often give the advice of, "Hey friend, what does your heart say?"

This saying derives from the belief that our heart knows best. Scripturally, though, the prophet Jeremiah warns us that the heart is deceitful above all other things. We all must know this is true. Whether young or old, we have all had an instance where our "heart" wanted something that wouldn't have been good for us or our future.

Galatians 5: 16-18 says this, *So I say, walk by the Spirit, and you will not gratify the desires of the flesh. For the flesh desires what is contrary to the Spirit, and the Spirit what is contrary to the flesh. They are in conflict with each other, so that you are not to do whatever you want. But if you are led by the Spirit, you are not under the law.*

Simply put, friend, be led by the Spirit, and not by our achy breaky heart. How do we do that? Well, the good news is that as we spend time with God and fall more deeply in love with Him, the more our heart's desires will line up with His.

Prayer:

Lord, search my heart and know me. Today I surrender my heart and its ways to you. Lead me by your Spirit and show me more of what that really looks like. All I want today is to know you more and to please your heart over mine. Amen.

DAY 20 - HEROES AND VILLAINS

For the righteous falls seven times and rises again, but the wicked stumble in times of calamity. (Proverbs 24:16)

I once heard a quote through social media that was a big perspective shift for me in how I could handle the pain from my past:

"A hero and a villain have one thing in common, pain. The difference is in how they handled that pain."

I don't know who first originated this quote, but my reason for sharing this quote is because it is a great example for today's scripture above. The story of heroes and villains, as we see in popular superhero movies, is a great analogy to the battles between the wicked and the righteous in the Bible. What are the differences between the wicked and the righteous?

The wicked reject God. They pursue the lusts of the flesh. They seek themselves. In contrast, the righteous pick up their cross and deny themselves, becoming more like Jesus every day. Although being wicked or being righteous seem far apart on the spectrum, there is a commonality that unites both. Pain. Whether someone is labeled wicked or someone is labeled righteous, they share this, their common humanity.

As discussed on Day 15, Jesus warns us that we will have troubles in this world, and He encourages us to take heart. Being human, we all have felt pain. We will go on feeling pain. What we do amid that pain determines our future. Are we going to stay down like the wicked described in Proverbs 24, or are we going to get back up?

Yeah, it may be the 8th time you have fallen, but you got back up! That's what separates the heroes from the villains. Today, I want to ask you, "What will you choose?"

Before ending this day, I want to make sure I speak to the person who may have stayed down. The person who may have found themselves in a pit and thinks there's no way out. I want to encourage you that, no matter where you are, you are not too far gone.

It may feel like getting up is impossible, but through Jesus, you too can get up and walk.

Prayer:

Lord, I recognize my pain and today choose to acknowledge and embrace it. You have seen everything I've been through, and I know that you have never left my side. Thank you for helping me to get back up to pursue you with all of my heart.

Amen.

DAY 21 - TAKING UP YOUR MAT

When Jesus saw their faith, he said to the paralyzed man, "Son, your sins are forgiven." Now some teachers of the law were sitting there, thinking to themselves, "Why does this fellow talk like that? He's blaspheming! Who can forgive sins but God alone?" Immediately Jesus knew in his spirit that this was what they were thinking in their hearts, and he said to them, "Why are you thinking these things? Which is easier: to say to this paralyzed man, 'Your sins are forgiven,' or to say, 'Get up, take your mat and walk'? But I want you to know that the Son of Man has authority on earth to forgive sins." So he said to the man, "I tell you, get up, take your mat and go home." He got up, took his mat and walked out in full view of them all. This amazed everyone and they praised God, saying, "We have never seen anything like this!" (Mark 2:5-12)

Today, I wanted to elaborate further on yesterday's devotional. Specifically, on those who may feel stuck in a pit and feel like getting up is impossible. This verse is burning on my heart to share with the person who is feeling like that. This passage of scripture is about more than just a man who was healed from his crippled state. I know this because, before that miracle took place, Jesus first said to the man, "Son, your sins are forgiven."

Why did Jesus say that?

Well, Jesus was speaking to a more important ailment than an ailment of the body. This man didn't just walk out of his crippled state. He also walked away from his untold past sins.

I also really want to home in on Jesus's command for the man to pick up his mat. Yes, it is a symbolic representation of the man leaving what he was bound to because of his crippling state... but... it does go even deeper than that.

Later, in the Gospel of Mark, chapter 8 to be exact, Jesus said this; "Whoever desires to come after Me, let him deny himself, and take up his cross, and follow Me."

Doesn't that sound very similar to Jesus's command to the man who was paralyzed? It was more than just a coincidence.

TAKING UP YOUR MAT

We all have or have been in the crippling state of being bound to sin. Lost and confused, blinded by our fleshly desire. But, just like the paralytic man, Jesus calls all of us to pick up our mat, also known as our cross, and follow Him.

If you are that person who feels crippled by sin, who feels stuck, know that through Jesus, you too can pick up your mat and walk again.

Prayer:

Jesus, today through you I pick up my cross and die to myself. I die to follow you with all that I am. Thank you for picking me up from my crippling state and setting me back on my feet to walk again towards you.

Amen.

DAY 22 - SEEK FIRST

But seek first the kingdom of God and His righteousness, and all these things will be added. (Matthew 6:34)

Before writing this day of our devotional, the song "This is the kingdom" by Elevation Worship has been on repeat. I'd been singing this song all day! There's a particular verse of the lyrics that I would like to share with you:

"Seek first the kingdom and all shall be added."

These words, that came straight from Jesus's mouth, has been encouraging me and lifting me up all day today. I want to encourage you with it as well.

If we're not careful, we can find ourselves in a place where we only see what's right in front of us, and nothing else. When we get to that place, it gets much harder to see God. Let this verse be a call to search in your very heart and ask, "What is really my first priority?"

SEEK FIRST

That question can be answered by realizing where we most keep our attention. Is our attention more on the things of the world, or is it on God and His kingdom? Are we more focused on being rich, or the wealth of His righteousness? Being more like Him every day should be our first focus. God is doing the same for us! He sees you right where you are, my friend. You are His child.

He has His eyes on the Sparrow, how much more are His eyes on you?

He dresses the lilies, how much more will He clothe you?

He doesn't owe us anything, He's God. We were created to be His. Not to build our own kingdoms.

Prayer:

God, search my heart and know me. Reveal the areas in which you have been made second. You are the very reason for this very breath that I just breathed. I want you first. I want to be more like you above all else.

DAY 23 - WONDERLESS

For ever since the world was created, people have seen the earth and sky. Through everything God made, they can clearly see his invisible qualities — his eternal power and divine nature. So they have no excuse for not knowing God. (Romans 1:24)

Have you ever lived through a day that no matter how bright the sun was, all you saw was gray? That may even be your day today.

I have too.

It's not like we become colorblind, but blind to the beauty around us. There has been a moment recently (while writing this book) that I was stuck in my head and everything around me just felt foggy...

I identify this phenomenon as a prison called gray. It is just that. A place in our minds that we become imprisoned to by our own vain imaginations; where the color that surrounds us begins to fade. We either ponder on the things that have happened and play it back in our minds like a movie as if it was on repeat, over-analyzing every word said and every choice made. In this prison, we even ponder on things that didn't happen, words we'd wished we'd said and choices we wished we'd made.

Where did the wonder go?

This verse in Romans reminds us that the beauty and the majesty of God's workmanship is all around us. It's even inside us.

Right now as you read this book, you have 78 organs and 37.2 trillion cells (according to Google) in your body working together, keeping you alive. Currently, we're on a planet full of life and creation, spinning around in the milky way, all being held together by its maker.

I don't know about you, but I refuse to live another day blinded to the beauty that is all around us. This truth hit me like a ton of bricks and screamed to me that it is time to WAKE UP! There is so much more to life than what I am living. Let's not remain stuck in this prison of gray when we have all of this color surrounding us.

Why live wonderless when we live in a world that is wonder-full?

Prayer:

God, you are glorious, and I worship you. Thank you for your creation and the reminder it is of your beauty and sovereignty. Your majesty is in every sunset, every smile, every bird's tweet, in the sound of the ocean's wave, in the glimmer of light when it touches the trees, in the wind that dances through my hair, in the hug of a loved one, in this next breath that I didn't even have to think about taking – It's all for your glory! There is no more place for me in the prison of gray in your masterpiece that is so full of color.

Amen.

DAY 24 - MOLDY OR MOLDED?

You will say to me then, "Why does he still find fault? For who can resist his will?" But who are you, O man, to answer back to God? Will what is molded say to its molder, "Why have you made me like this?" Has the potter no right over the clay, to make out of the same lump one vessel for honorable use and another for dishonorable use? What if God, desiring to show his wrath and to make known his power, has endured with much patience vessels of wrath prepared for destruction, in order to make known the riches of his glory for vessels of mercy, which he has prepared beforehand for glory — even us whom he has called, not from the Jews only but also from the Gentiles? (Romans 9:19-24)

One night, a friend called me in a state they described as feeling moldy. Honestly, I have never heard of that term used in that way, but it described exactly what I was feeling too. In that conversation, I felt useless, because I too was in that state.

MOLDY OR MOLDED?

As the conversation went on, I shared my heart on what feeling moldy felt like. Mold grows in unkept damp places in houses, and in food that stays out for too long. In this life, feeling moldy is inevitable. Each one of us is growing older, and our bodies are degrading every hour. One day, Lord willing, we will both be old. Our joints and bones won't work the same. Our skin will sag, and our eyes will have bags so big that we could go grocery shopping with em.

As I was saying all of this to my friends, God spoke something into my heart. Are we moldy or being molded?

This verse elaborates on this question perfectly. Being molded in the hands of the potter has a romantic tone to it, but it also hurts. The potter must squeeze and crush to be able to form. I'm not saying God's intention is to crush you, but I am saying that He will take the moment in which life feels like it's crushing you and use it to form you into someone stronger and wiser than you were before.

Yeah, we're all getting older. Yeah, one day we will have to walk through death's door. Are we going to waste this life molding, or are we going to allow God to have His way and mold us into the new creation He promised to make us?

Prayer:

Lord I am yours, mold me and shape me how you please, to look and live more like you. Amen.

DAY 25 – EXITING TEMPTATION STATION

Then Jesus was led up by the Spirit into the wilderness to be tempted by the devil. 2 And when He had fasted forty days and forty nights, afterward He was hungry. 3 Now when the tempter came to Him, he said, "If You are the Son of God, command that these stones become bread." But He answered and said, "It is written, 'Man shall not live by bread alone, but by every word that proceeds from the mouth of God.'" (Matthew 4:1-11)

Temptation station?

"What is that?", You so validly ask.

Temptation station is where we all find ourselves at one point or another. Even as little kids, we can find ourselves tempted to put our hand in the cookie jar. Is it wrong that we have been at that station before?

No. It's not a sin to be tempted. It's a sin when we buy the temptation ticket and let it take us farther than we want to go and make us stay longer than we wanted to stay.

EXITING TEMPTATION STATION

Even Jesus found Himself at temptation station. In today's scripture, Jesus has just been baptized and was led by the Spirit out into the wilderness. Without having eaten anything for 40 nights, and basically at the brink of death, He was tempted by Satan to turn the dry stones into fresh bread. You may think that wasn't a bad suggestion to do.

After all, what could be wrong with fresh bread?

The enemy is cunning. Yet, he's not too cunning for Jesus. The real point of the temptation of the bread was to find the saving source in something else other than God the father. This is why Jesus fights the temptation with the word of God by saying,

"It is written, 'Man shall not live by bread alone, but by every word that proceeds from the mouth of God.'"

At that moment, Jesus was in temptation station. He didn't buy the ticket. He didn't turn the stones into bread. Rather, He became our bread of life, in whom we are fully satisfied.

You may be thinking, "Well, He's Jesus, fully God and fully human, of course He didn't sin."

One of my favorite aspects of this scripture is that yes, God is fully God, but He chose to counter this temptation in a fully human way. And He did this by using the word of God. Jesus countered this temptation in a way that everyone could as well, by using the word of God. So that's the solution!

Anytime you may find yourself in temptation station...

Don't punch the ticket...

Use the word of God!

Prayer:

God, thank you that in you, I have everything I need. You satisfy every longing in my heart. More than anything the enemy, my flesh, or this world has to offer me... You are better. I receive your freedom that was bought for me by the price of your blood, and I choose to exit temptation station and instead take the narrow road into your Presence.

Amen.

DAY 26 - SCISSORS TO FEATHERS

Death and life are in the power of the tongue, And those who love it will eat its fruit. (Proverbs 18:21)

At the time of writing today's devotional, I have switched jobs three times. It's crazy because I had a job for six years, and now I'm at this place where everything has been shifting. I am currently a Middle School Teaching Assistant. I've only been there for a little over a month, but in my short time there, I have learned so much.

One thing I've learned is that the middle school age is one of the most crucial ages in someone's life.

Why is that? Well, this is the age where they stop believing that they can fly. Remember the days when we thought we were superheroes, rock stars, or the best singer on the planet? The days we would dress up and dream of going to the moon? What happens to that belief that anything is possible? How do our dreams get crushed?

SCISSORS TO FEATHERS

With every person, I believe it's different. For some, it could be trauma. For others, it could be just growing up. There is a saying that we are all products of our environment.

When I observe my middle school students compared to the elementary students that I get to interact with, I hear, "I can't", more from the middle school students. I hear, "I can", more from the elementary school students.

How does this change take place - from being able to fly like a bird to not even being able to believe that they could complete a math problem?

The scissor to their feathers is in their words. It's ok to trim our feathers with our words a little bit. In fact, it's healthy, and it's called facing reality. But there is a difference between facing reality and putting your dreams to death.

Jesus puts it like this, "For truly I tell you, if you have faith the size of a mustard seed, you will say to this mountain, 'Move from here to there,' and it will move; and nothing will be impossible for you." (Matthew 17:20-21).

When we change our words, we change our life. It isn't that we can instantly become millionaires by just saying it. It's rather the instilling in us of a belief that helps us change and shift our habits to one day accomplish our biggest dreams. Our words are the foundation of our future.

Have you cut your own feathers too much? Have you let someone else take their scissors to your feathers? If so, counteract them with God's word today:

And the LORD will make you the head and not the tail; you shall be above only, and not be beneath, if you heed the commandments of the LORD your God, which I command you today, and are careful to observe them. (Deuteronomy 28:13)

For I know the plans I have for you," declares the LORD, "plans to prosper you and not to harm you, plans to give you hope and a future. (Jeremiah 29:11)

I praise you because I am fearfully and wonderfully made; your works are wonderful, I know that full well. (Psalm 139:14)

I can do all things through Christ who strengthens me. (Philippians 4:13)

SCISSORS TO FEATHERS

God is a redeemer. I proclaim over you today, as you speak God's words over yourself, that feathers will begin to grow again. Put the scissors away, and don't allow anyone else access to your feathers again. It's time to fly!

Prayer:

(For our prayer today, I encourage you to simply speak the verses above over yourself. Only you know the trauma and deadly words that have been spoken over you. Spend time with God today, and with the faith of a mustard seed, allow Him the access to restore your wings.)

DAY 27 - FIRM FOUNDATION

"Therefore, whoever hears these sayings of Mine, and does them, I will liken him to a wise man who built his house on the rock: 25 and the rain descended, the floods came, and the winds blew and beat on that house; and it did not fall, for it was founded on the rock. "But everyone who hears these sayings of Mine, and does not do them, will be like a foolish man who built his house on the sand: 27 and the rain descended, the floods came, and the winds blew and beat on that house; and it fell. And great was its fall." (Matthew 7:24-27)

Today's verse hits home hard.

I hope it's okay that I get a little bit personal today, because this is a verse that I wrestled with a lot in my ex-fiancé and I's break up. This was the theme for our wedding. That God is our foundation on which our marriage would be built, like a house on the rock.

Around three months before our wedding, I was in shock when I found myself sitting alone in the rubble & dust of the fallen house that was our relationship.

FIRM FOUNDATION

It didn't work out. As I was holding on to the pieces of our "house", I became so confused as to why something that was built on His love, and was carefully handled to please Him, would fall apart the way it did.

In my confusion and brokenness, God gave me this revelation. Yes, building a house on the rock makes the foundation so strong that storms that come won't be able to tear it down. But what happens when you leave the stove on? Even a house built on a firm foundation can burn into flames when neglected.

The house of our relationship burned down, but because God and His word was the foundation of my whole life, I still had a firm foundation to stand and start building on again. Sometimes we can blame God for the things that other people, the enemy, or even our own selves do. Yet even on the darkest day, God is still good. Even when we fall, He is there to pick us back up. Let this be a reminder, that how you build something matters. Build your life on God and His word.

It doesn't mean everything will be perfect, because humans aren't perfect, except for Jesus. But if everything we build crumbles and falls, God will always be there. This world is but a vapor, but God is forever.

Prayer:

Lord, be my center and my foundation. Search me and examine my heart. If there is anything I am putting my trust in other than you, help me to re-prioritize where my foundation is and to build my life on you, my rock. Amen.

DAY 28 – THE GOOD OL' DAYS

"Show me, LORD, my life's end and the number of my days; let me know how fleeting my life is. You have made my days a mere handbreadth; the span of my years is as nothing before you. Everyone is but a breath," (Psalm 39:4-5)

When I say the word nostalgia, what do you think of?

Growing up, I would hear my parents talk about movies they grew up with, games they used to play, and hairstyles they used to have. I was confused listening to them reminisce because all I knew was the now. Now, being 28 years old…. I get it.

I get nostalgic when I see videos on social media about the red and yellow car, old Nickelodeon cartoons, the Game Boy, Disney VHS movies, Happy Meal Toys, Silver pencil sharpeners, and the old videogame isles that stores had. Remembering those things just hits me and makes me miss the "Good Ole Days." Yet, it was when we were in them that we were so fixated on the future.

THE GOOD OL' DAYS

As this verse from the Psalms tells us, life is fleeting. What if we are living in the good ole days right now? Are we watching them slip by, or are we making the most of every moment? Let's be thankful for where we are and give God praise for the present.

We have His gift of living.

Prayer:

God, thank you for this present day that I get to open up and enjoy. Honestly, I miss the simplicity of then, but I am grateful that you gave me the now. Help me see the beauty and wonder of today.

Amen.

DAY 29 - BLESSED

Now when Jesus saw the crowds, he went up on a mountainside and sat down. His disciples came to him, and he began to teach them. He said: "Blessed are the poor in spirit, for theirs is the kingdom of heaven. Blessed are those who mourn, for they will be comforted. Blessed are the meek, for they will inherit the earth. Blessed are those who hunger and thirst for righteousness, for they will be filled. Blessed are the merciful, for they will be shown mercy. Blessed are the pure in heart, for they will see God. Blessed are the peacemakers, for they will be called children of God. Blessed are those who are persecuted because of righteousness, for theirs is the kingdom of heaven. "Blessed are you when people insult you, persecute you, and falsely say all kinds of evil against you because of me. Rejoice and be glad, because great is your reward in heaven, for in the same way they persecuted the prophets who were before you. (Matthew 5:1-12)

Blessed. Usually, we use that term when we have everything we could have only dreamed of. For some, blessed could be a big house and an expensive car. This use of the word goes back to Bible times, maybe not with a car, but meaning a materialistic object. Jesus does not mean it that way. He is forever changing the game: He said blessed are those who mourn, the poor in spirit, and those who are persecuted! Doesn't that seem upside down? That's exactly what He did with this sermon – He overturned it all.

No matter what our social economic status says, we are blessed. It's not some positivity brainwash, but what Jesus provides here is truth. He points out the hardship and circumstantial challenges people are potentially facing, but He also provides the perspective that, through God, we are blessed. We have all that we need in Him. The realization that God fulfilling our innermost desire is one of the first steps of living the best day of our life.

Prayer:

Lord, I can have a relationship with you; I am blessed. You fulfill every desire of my soul, and although my circumstances may not always be where I imagine them, you are with me, and that is more than enough to call myself blessed and highly favored.

DAY 30 - MUCH LOVE

"There was a certain creditor who had two debtors. One owed five hundred denarii, and the other fifty. And when they had nothing with which to repay, he freely forgave them both. Tell Me, therefore, which of them will love him more?" Simon answered and said, "I suppose the one whom he forgave more." And He said to him, "You have rightly judged." Then He turned to the woman and said to Simon, "Do you see this woman? I entered your house; you gave Me no water for My feet, but she washed My feet with her tears and wiped them with the hair of her head. you gave Me no kiss, but this woman has not ceased to kiss My feet since the time I came in. You did not anoint My head with oil, but this woman has anointed My feet with fragrant oil. Therefore, I say to you, her sins, which are many, are forgiven, for she loved much. But to whom little is forgiven, the same loves little." Then He said to her, "Your sins are forgiven." And those who sat at the table with Him began to say to themselves, "Who is this who even forgives sins?" Then He said to the woman, "Your faith has saved you. Go in peace." (Luke 7 41-50)

MUCH LOVE

For today's devotional, this scripture said all that needed to be said. Those who have been shown much love, love much.

Prayer:

In today's prayer, I want you in your own words to pray and reflect on how He has loved and forgiven you much. Then,

"Go in peace."

DAY 31 - THE TWO-SIDED COIN

Death and life are in the power of the tongue, And those who love it will eat its fruit. (Proverbs 18:21)

We just read this verse together a few days ago, but I wanted to revisit it for today's topic: The power of the tongue is like a double-sided coin. On one side of this coin you have life (heads). On the other side you have death (tails).

This double-sided coin, our words, will determine the trajectory of our every day and thus our lives. There is power in our words, in speaking things into existence. Speaking into existence isn't about saying some hocus pocus faking it until you make it mumbo jumbo. It's about understanding the fruit or toxicity the coin has over your life.

One side says: One day,

The other side says: Day one

One side says: I'm stupid

The other side says: I'm learning

THE TWO-SIDED COIN

One side says: I'm a failure

The other side says: I just made a mistake

One side says: I'm tired

The other side says: I'm alive.

Carry a quarter, or some other coin, in your wallet and or purse. When you feel some type of way, in need of some direction to lead your feelings for example, take that coin out, look at both sides, and consider the outcomes on each side. Then lay the coin down on the direction you feel led to go. Life is not just a coin toss; it's a choice to speak from one of two sides. Heads or tails. Life or death.

Will you choose life?

If you said yes, bring your choice to God in prayer, claiming victory over death. It's not just one day... It's day one.

Prayer:

God, thank you for being my power against every evil thought that comes against my mind. I take it captive today and choose this freedom you gave me to speak life over myself and everyone that comes into my influence today.

In Jesus's name. Amen.

THE BEGINNING

See then that you walk circumspectly, not as fools but as wise, redeeming the time, because the days are evil. Therefore, do not be unwise, but understand what the will of the Lord is. And do not be drunk with wine, in which is dissipation; but be filled with the Spirit, speaking to one another in psalms and hymns and spiritual songs, singing and making melody in your heart to the Lord, giving thanks always for all things to God the Father in the name of our Lord Jesus Christ, submitting to one another in the fear of God. (Ephesians 5:15-21)

You finally made it to the beginning.

That's right, this is the beginning! My hope is that, even if you are reading this at the age of 72, you would recognize that as long as you have breath in your lungs, it's not too late to live the best day of your life for God.

Life is not about how young you are, how good you've been, or how good you have it. It's about how good He is and living every day with Him. He is the redeemer of our

THE BEGINNING

lives, but also be encouraged by this, He is also the redeemer of our time.

The reason I made this devotional 31 days, and not 365, is because I hope that someone could begin this book without a habit of reading God's word but leave this devotional diving deeper into God's word daily. Allow God's word to be your roadmap; follow the leading of His Spirit.

Yeah, life may not all be sunshine and rainbows, but it is life and life more abundant. While you're in the present, you might as well open it.

For our final prayer, I would like to pray for you!

The Final Prayer:

God, thank you for your child who either has read this book all the way through, or even if this prayer is the first thing they chose to read from this book. I pray that right now they will begin to feel your very real and life-giving presence; that they will feel a sense of peace that you are with them and for them. Quiet any thoughts of doubt or fear. As they come to you today, let them feel refreshed and new. Guide them through your word as they consistently seek you from it.

I pray that your words will become living and breathing to them. Release any scales that may be over their spiritual eyes and break down any walls from the enemy that is holding them back from you. As they come humbly before you, fill them. Fill every hole in their heart, piece back together every crack in their heart and mold them to be more like you for your glory alone.

I speak your blessings over them, their family, their friends, over everyone they meet. No matter the circumstance, I pray that they will always see the gift in this day that you have made. I pray that their trust may always be with you, as you are faithfully good and upright.

Thank you, Lord, for the opportunity to write this book, I pray that you would take these words, written by human hands, and use them for your glory to impact your kingdom.

Let your will be done. In Jesus name, Amen.

DAY 0 - ZERO

Though a righteous man falls seven times, he will get up, but the wicked will stumble into ruin. (Proverbs 24:16)

Surprise!

I felt led to create one more day of this devotional. This one is different from the rest. The purpose of it is found in the name: It's for the one who has found themselves in need of a fresh start.

Maybe it's been 30 years since you have read this devotional and have lost the joy you once felt. Maybe it's only been a week since completing this book and you are struggling with consistency in your relationship with God... This day is a place for you to find a restart. And not just any restart... Restart Himself. Jesus is our constant restart.

Because of the LORD's faithful love we do not perish, for His mercies never end. They are new every morning; great is your faithfulness! I say, *"The LORD is my portion, therefore I will put my hope in him."* (Lamentations 3:22-24)

ZERO

Good news, His mercies were made new this morning. Jesus still loves you, and you are still a son and daughter of God. Yes, you may have fallen seven times, but it's time to get up for the eighth.

For his anger lasts only a moment, but his favor, a lifetime. Weeping may stay overnight, but there is joy in the morning. (Psalm 30:5)

There is Joy this morning. You are cleansed, free and whole in Him. You are washed white as snow.

Prayer:

For this day's prayer, I want you to read Psalms 25 in your own Bible and spend time sharing your heart with Him. He wants to share His heart with you too, and it is this: God loved the world in this way: He gave his one and only Son, so that everyone who believes in Him will not perish but have eternal life.

It's time to begin anew!

THE THANKS-A-BUNCH! PAGE

There are a bunch of people who have supported me and/or worked on this book that I would like to say a big Thanks-A-Bunch to. Firstly, the biggest of thank you's is to God for being our Creator and Heavenly Father. This book wouldn't have existed, and we wouldn't have existed either, without Him.

I'm thankful for His unconditional love that never gave up on me and decided to mold me more like Him with each day He has gifted us with. I am also thankful that He doesn't always call the qualified. I in no way thought that I was qualified to write this book, but it was through His Spirit that it was birthed and written, all for His glory and to reach His people.

Secondly, I would like to thank all of my family and friends who supported me through this long 2-year journey in writing a devotional that only takes a month to read (lol). I almost gave up a few times, but their encouragement, love, and belief in this book helped me push through and helped it become what it is today. To each and everyone of you... Thank you. And a specific thank you to my immediate family: Bonnie, Eddie, Barbara, Richard, Gabrielle, Oscar, and Jorden. Thank you for everything.

Thirdly, I would like to thank my good friend Nick who created the hot air balloon logo. I knew I wanted something with balloons, but he knew about my love for hot air balloons and suggested we went that route. I'm so glad that he did. There is a personal reason for it as well, and the fact that he knew me that well to suggest that and being willing to use his talents to make it come to life, he really is a real one. Thank you, Nick.

Fourthly, I would like to thank another good friend, Austin, and shout out his business, Collect & Contrast. He helped design the cover and made it look more appealing. I'm so thankful he was willing to use his gift to help the book look as clean as it does. To find out more about his awesome services, follow him on Instagram: @collect_contrast

Fifthly, I want to thank my amazing publisher, Choice Publications led by Joseph Lawrence. It is a total God thing that our paths encountered. Without him, this book would not have had a possibility to be published. Choice publications has worked hard in making HTBDOYL exist and I could not be more grateful that God lined me up with this great publishing company. If you would like to find out more information on them, there is a whole page in this book (page 123) that is dedicated to promoting their services.

Lastly, but certainly not least, thank *you* for taking your time in reading this book. You are the reason and the purpose why God had me write and publish this book. All to tell you that He loves you and to encourage you in your personal walk with Him.

Time is precious. The fact that you took the chance to spend a month of it on this book blows my mind and is not to be taken lightly.

To you, thank you.

A MESSAGE FROM THE PUBLISHER

Bringing this wonderful book to publication has been a great delight to me and to all of us at Choice Publications. I first met my good friend Nicholas in college at Southeastern University; I was struck by his positivity and outgoingness. After college, we lost touch.

Then, one day, we both happened to be teaching at the same school in Central Florida. That providential meeting led to the book you are holding today. Ever since my Grandad started this publishing house, we have strived to remain humble and teachable for the Lord to work through us – how wonderfully He did so with that chance meeting and reunion!

Our mission at Choice is to bring to life the books that matter, the books that change lives, open hearts, and expand minds. I would be honored if you would visit our website, **choicepublications.com** , to see for yourself our diverse catalog of books, and/or to inquire about our publishing process, if you are seeking publication.

~Joseph Lawrence (CEO)

THE END... FOR REAL THIS TIME!

You have finally made it to the real end of the book. If you're reading this, thank you for making it this far and for sticking with this book. I would like to end this book on the best note possible, by praying Numbers 6:24-26 over you:

"May the LORD bless you and protect you;

may the LORD make his face shine on you

and be gracious to you;

may the LORD look with favor on you

and give you peace."

Numbers 6:24-26

HAVE THE BEST DAY OF YOUR LIFE!